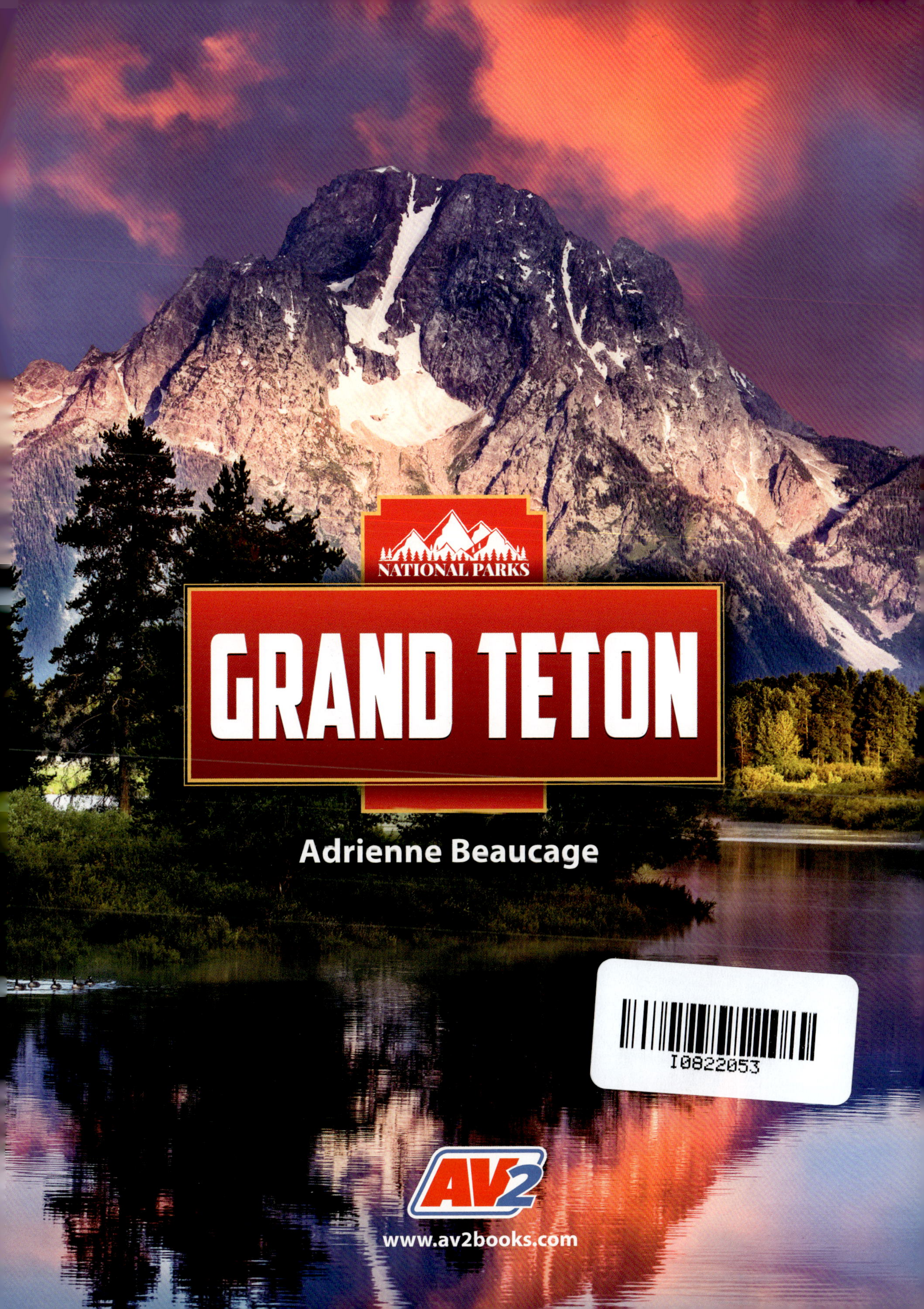
NATIONAL PARKS
GRAND TETON
Adrienne Beaucage
I0822053
AV2
www.av2books.com

Step 1
Go to **www.av2books.com**

Step 2
Enter this unique code
TWLUCPEK5

Step 3
Explore your interactive eBook!

AV2 is optimized for use on any device

Your interactive eBook comes with...

Contents
Browse a live contents page to easily navigate through resources

Audio
Listen to sections of the book read aloud

Videos
Watch informative video clips

Weblinks
Gain additional information for research

Slideshows
View images and captions

Try This!
Complete activities and hands-on experiments

Key Words
Study vocabulary, and complete a matching word activity

Quizzes
Test your knowledge

Share
Share titles within your Learning Management System (LMS) or Library Circulation System

Citation
Create bibliographical references following the Chicago Manual of Style

This title is part of our AV2 digital subscription

1-Year 3–8 Subscription
ISBN 978-1-7911-3306-1

Access hundreds of AV2 titles with our digital subscription.
Sign up for a FREE trial at **www.av2books.com/trial**

CONTENTS

A Striking Landscape

Grand Teton National Park, in northwestern Wyoming, is best known for its dramatic mountain peaks. The rugged Teton mountain range shoots up from the ground in a way that appears to defy gravity. The stark beauty of the mountains is complemented by the park's shimmering lakes and rivers, serene meadows, and rich array of wildlife.

This majestic landscape took billions of years to form. Glaciers, **erosion**, and earthquakes all contributed to shaping the mountains and valleys that make up the park. Even though the Teton Range is one of North America's youngest mountain ranges, it contains some of the oldest rocks on the continent.

Grand Teton National Park covers an area of about **310,000 acres** (125,000 hectares).

At **13,775 feet** (4,200 meters), **Grand Teton** is the highest peak in the Teton Range.

Grand Teton is the **only U.S. national park** to have a **commercial airport** located entirely within its borders.

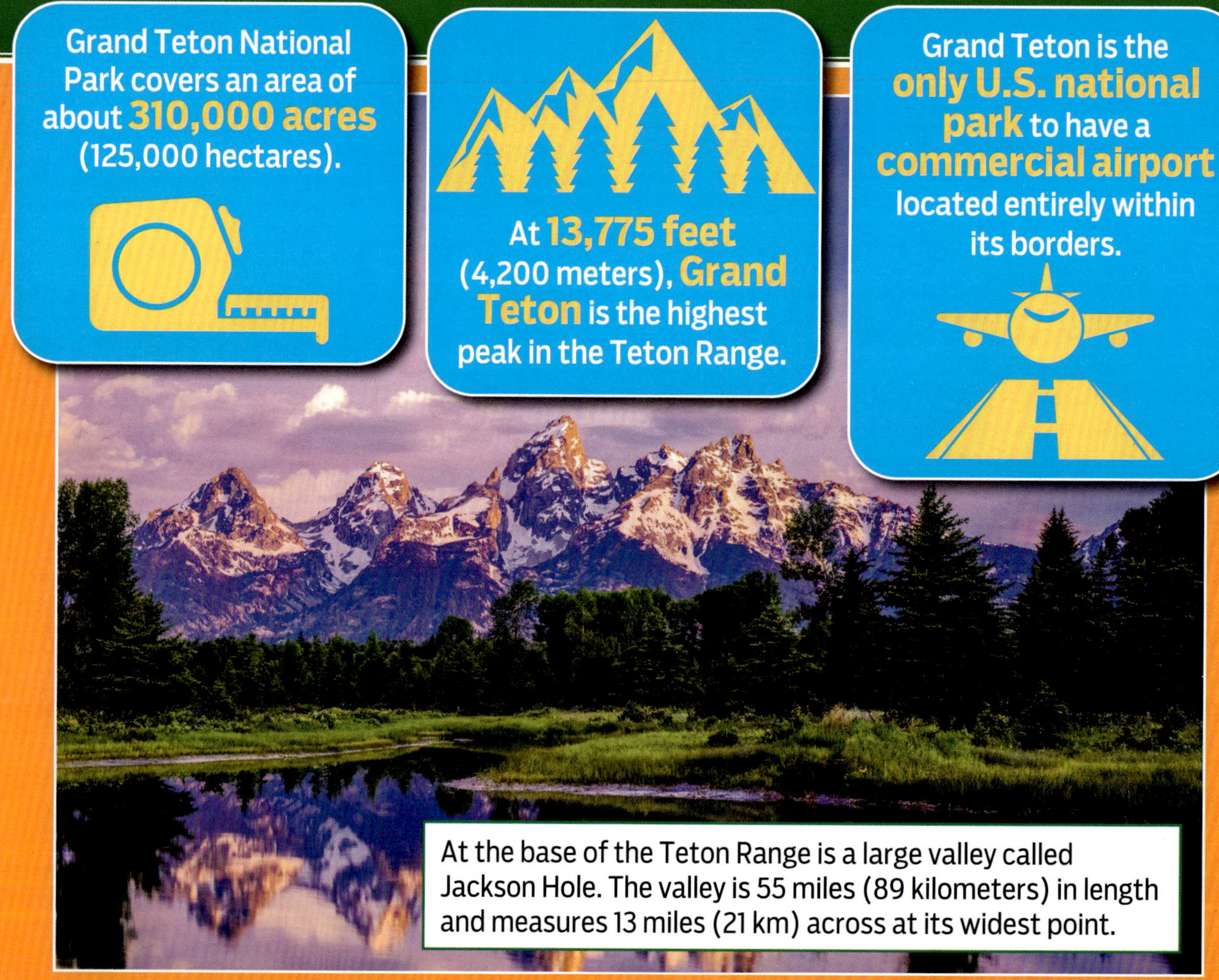

At the base of the Teton Range is a large valley called Jackson Hole. The valley is 55 miles (89 kilometers) in length and measures 13 miles (21 km) across at its widest point.

Grand Teton's stunning scenery has long drawn adventurers to the area, a tradition that continues to this day. With more than 3 million visitors annually, Grand Teton is among the top 10 most visited national parks in the United States. People come to the park to hike its picturesque valleys, kayak its quiet lakes, and take sightseeing drives along its many scenic roads.

Incredible views abound along Grand Teton's more than 200 miles (322 km) of hiking trails.

MAPPING GRAND TETON

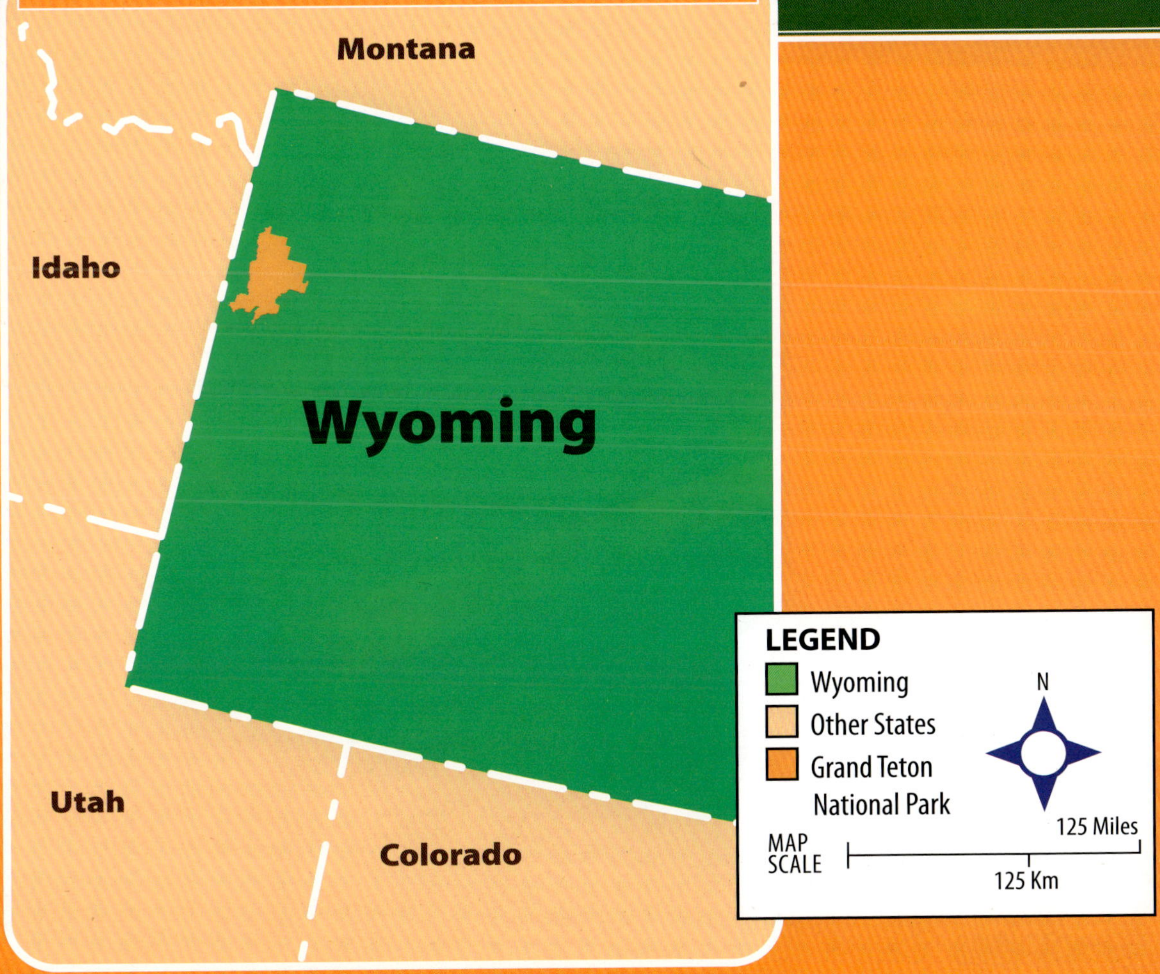

Where Is Grand Teton?

Grand Teton National Park is located just south of Wyoming's other national park, Yellowstone. The two parks are connected by the John D. Rockefeller, Jr. Memorial Parkway. About 24 miles (39 km) south of Grand Teton is Jackson, a town of about 10,500 people. Cheyenne, the capital city of Wyoming, is 416 miles (669 km) southeast of the park.

The Teton Range is part of a larger range called the Rocky Mountains, or Rockies. The Rockies stretch for 3,000 miles (4,828 km), all the way from northern Alberta and British Columbia in Canada down to New Mexico in the United States. They include more than 100 individual ranges, which are divided into four groups based on their **physiography** and **geology**. The Teton Range is part of the Middle Rockies grouping.

In some places, the Rockies are more than 300 miles (483 km) wide.

PUZZLER

Grand Teton National Park includes much of the Rockies' Teton Range. Stretches of the Rocky Mountains can be found in several other U.S. national parks as well.

Q: Can you identify each of these national parks on the map below? All feature sections of the Rocky Mountains.

A Trip Back in Time

The Tetons were not always part of the area's landscape. About 85 million years ago, the area where the Tetons now stand was covered by a large inland sea. Lying deep beneath this sea were gneiss and granite, rocks that would later form the Teton Range. Over a period of 25 million years, the sea began to retreat, and the Rocky Mountains started to rise. The rocks of the Teton Range, however, remained hidden beneath Earth's surface.

Starting about 10 million years ago, a series of massive earthquakes began. These earthquakes were triggered by movement along the Teton **fault**. They tilted the mountain block and pushed it upwards, while dropping the valley floor. This activity created the Teton Range.

Glaciers have also shaped and sculpted Grand Teton's landscape. Approximately 2 million years ago, large pieces of ice flowed into the valley. They cut into the land, creating U-shaped canyons, knife-like ridges, and the other glacial features for which the Tetons are now known.

The U-shaped Cascade Canyon was created by past glacial activity in the area.

BILLIONS OF YEARS IN THE MAKING

The geologic history of the Teton Range began approximately 2.7 billion years ago. Mud, sand, and other **sediments** were deposited into the sea, where they were buried up to 20 miles (32 km) deep. Pressure and heat caused the sediment to turn into gneiss, which is a type of **metamorphic rock**.

Gneiss contains layers that look like zebra stripes.

The granite found within the Tetons started to form about 2.5 billion years ago as a result of volcanic activity. **Magma** squeezed into cracks within the gneiss. As the magma cooled, it formed crystals and turned into granite.

Together, gneiss and granite make up the Teton Range. While most of the range is made from gneiss, it is granite that forms the highest peaks in the central Teton Range. This includes Grand Teton itself.

Granite is an igneous rock. This is rock that has been formed by the cooling and hardening of magma.

Plant Life

More than 1,000 **species** of plants can be found in Grand Teton National Park and its surrounding area. Wildflowers bloom in the warmer months of May to September, while other plants grow year-round. Several plant communities have formed based on the conditions, such as moisture levels, elevation, and the soil, in different regions of the park.

The ridges, canyons, and mountainsides contain soil that is able to hold moisture. This makes it possible for trees to grow. Most of the trees in these areas are coniferous. Species include lodgepole pine, Engelmann spruce, and Douglas fir. Deciduous trees, such as aspens and cottonwoods, can be found growing in the moist soil along the park's lakeshores and rivers.

Grasses grow in every plant community in the park. Some of the most common grasses in Grand Teton include bearded wheatgrass and pinegrass. Grasses are important to the park because they help to stabilize the soil, holding it in place and creating a base on which other plants can grow. Grasses are also a primary food source for many of the park's animals, and are used by some animals to build and insulate their homes.

Arrowleaf balsamroot is a wildflower that grows throughout Grand Teton, in areas ranging from foothills to meadows to forests. Fields of these flowers typically appear in May and stay in bloom for a few weeks.

PLANT COMMUNITIES

Grand Teton is home to a variety of **ecosystems**, each with its own unique features. These features come together to create **habitats** in which different plants can grow. Plant communities are created when plant species with similar needs begin growing in the same area. Grand Teton has five main plant communities.

Alpine These communities are found high in the mountains, in areas known for their shallow soils and extreme temperature shifts. Most plants found here, including the alpine laurel, grow close to the ground.

Forests Trees gather in areas with moist soil. The forests they create can be found at elevations up to 10,000 feet (3,000 m). Other plants grow within Grand Teton's forest communities as well. These include heartleaf arnica and huckleberry bushes.

Meadows These communities are often found within other types of communities. Grasses and flowering plants are their main inhabitants. Elk thistle and mountain bluebells are just two of the plants that grow in Grand Teton's meadow communities.

Sagebrush Flats Sagebrush is the key plant found on Jackson Hole's valley floor. This plant grows well in the shallow, rocky soils there. Other plants that rely on these conditions include Indian paintbrush and silvery lupine.

Wetlands Plants that thrive on moisture are found in Grand Teton's swamp and marsh areas, as well as along its riverbanks. Pond lilies, monkey flowers, and willows are some of the plants that grow here.

Grand Teton Wildlife

Grand Teton National Park lies in the center of a much larger ecosystem called the Greater Yellowstone Ecosystem. This is one of the few remaining **temperate** ecosystems on Earth. The Greater Yellowstone Ecosystem spans more than 20 million acres (8.1 million ha). A wide variety of wildlife, ranging from mammals and birds to fish and amphibians, lives in or migrates to this region.

More than 300 species of birds visit or live in the park. One is the trumpeter swan, which is North America's largest waterfowl. The calliope hummingbird is another resident. It is North America's smallest bird. Other birds found in the park include the western bluebird, osprey, sage grouse, and bald eagle.

Badgers, wolverines, and long-tailed weasels are among the smaller mammals that make their home in the park. Large mammals include deer, bison, moose, elk, and antelope. The park is also home to **predatory** mammals such as wolves, mountain lions, black bears, and grizzly bears.

The greater sage grouse is one of Grand Teton's most iconic bird species. Its small population has been threatened in recent years by habitat loss.

THE PLIGHT OF THE GRIZZLY

Grizzly bears once roamed throughout the United States. Their range was significantly reduced as more and more people came from other parts of the world to settle on the land. It is estimated that the country had about 50,000 grizzlies in the early 1800s. By the 1950s, they were almost **extinct**. One of the few places they continued to live in was the Greater Yellowstone Ecosystem. Still, the population there consisted of fewer than 200 bears.

In 1973, the U.S. government passed the **Endangered** Species Act. This act provides protection to threatened wildlife populations. Animals listed on the country's endangered species list are given special allowances. They cannot be hunted. Their habitats must be protected. Plans must also be put in place to increase their populations.

The grizzly bear was one of the first animals to be put on the endangered species list. Since then, the population in and around Grand Teton National Park has grown. Today, it is estimated that there are as many as 750 grizzly bears in the Greater Yellowstone Ecosystem.

With its numbers becoming more stable, the grizzly bear's presence on the endangered species list has been under debate for the past few years.

Becoming Grand Teton

European settlers first arrived in the Grand Teton area in the late 1800s. When they found the land unsuitable for large-scale farming, they sought other ways to make an income. Several set up guest ranches for tourists from the east.

Soon, other businesses opened to take advantage of the tourist traffic. It was not long before people became worried that the area was losing its charm. In 1923, a group of area residents held a meeting to discuss plans for preserving the land. Their efforts paid off in 1929, with the creation of Grand Teton National Park.

The initial park was only about half of its current size. In 1926, John D. Rockefeller, Jr., a wealthy businessman, had visited Teton. He fell in love with the area's natural splendor and secretly began to buy large tracts of land. His plan was to buy as much land as he could and then donate it to the government so that it could be added it to the park.

President Grover Cleveland took the first step toward protecting the Teton region in 1897 by creating the Teton Forest Reserve. The area was expanded in 1908 to become Teton National Forest.

In 1930, it was revealed that Rockefeller was behind the secret land purchases. People protested the sales, saying that they had not been told that the land was going to become part of the park. It took several years to settle the disputes. Rockefeller was not able to donate the land until 1949. It became part of the park the next year, along with the Jackson Hole National Monument, forming the Grand Teton National Park known today.

BIOGRAPHY

John D. Rockefeller, Jr. (1874–1960)

Philanthropist John D. Rockefeller, Jr., was devoted to humanitarian causes. He helped create many large organizations to benefit others. These include the Rockefeller Institute for Medical Research, now known as Rockefeller University, and the United Service Organizations, an agency that provides services to members of the military. He also funded the construction of Manhattan's Rockefeller Center, helping create 75,000 jobs during the **Great Depression**.

Rockefeller felt strongly about **conservation**. He bought and donated significant parcels of land, contributing to the development of Shenandoah, Acadia, and Grand Teton National Parks. In 1972, Rockefeller was honored by Congress with the naming of the John D. Rockefeller, Jr. Memorial Parkway.

FACTS OF LIFE

Born: January 29, 1874

Hometown: Cleveland, Ohio

Occupation: Philanthropist

Died: May 11, 1960

THE BIG PICTURE

The Tetons are fault-block mountains. This type of mountain is formed when part of Earth's crust breaks, creating a fault line. The creation of the fault causes rock on one side of the line to be pushed up over the rock on the other side. The result is a fault-block mountain. Mountain ranges created through this process can be found in various parts of the world.

Sierra Nevada
United States

Atlantic Ocean

Pacific Ocean

Teton Range
United States

Southern Ocean

LEGEND
- Water
- Land
- Antarctica

N

MAP SCALE 0 — 2,000 Miles / 2,000 Km

Arctic Ocean
Harz Mountains
Germany
Europe
Asia
Pacific
Ocean
Africa
Indian
Ocean
Australia
Vindhya Range
India
West Sayan Range
Russia
Antarctica

People of the Tetons

As glaciers receded from the valley thousands of years ago, people began moving into the area. The earliest evidence of humans in the region is from at least 11,000 years ago. These people are known as Paleo Native Americans today.

At the time of European settlement, Native Americans in the area included the Bannock, Blackfoot, Crow, Shoshone, Flathead, Nez Perce, and Gros Ventre. These peoples set up seasonal camps near the region's lakes and rivers. From their camps, they would harvest berries and roots and hunt for wildlife. They also collected minerals and rocks. Most of the camps were in what is now the northern part of Grand Teton National Park. Native American groups would often leave the valley in the winter months, following the migrating wildlife.

Today, the Shoshone continue to live in the region. They work hard to preserve their language and cultural practices, and to pass them down to new generations.

Over time, the Shoshone developed permanent settlements along and in the Teton Range. This changed in the 1860s, when the U.S. government created the Wind River Reservation for them.

PUZZLER

Native Americans came to the Teton region largely because of the big game herds found in the area. They included animals such as bison, moose, and elk. Native Americans hunted these animals for both their skins and their meat.

Q. Why were the skins of animals important to Native Americans in the region?

ANSWER: Animal skins were used to create warm clothing, which was needed to survive the cold winter months.

TIMELINE

25 million years ago
The Rocky Mountains start to form.

11,000 years ago
Paleo Native Americans move into the region.

25 million years ago

10 million years ago

1810

1890

10 million years ago
The Teton Range begins to rise due to earthquake activity.

1810
European fur trappers arrive in the area.

1884
European settlers establish the first permanent community in the area. Tourists start visiting the region soon after.

1929
Grand Teton National Park is created. At this time, it includes only the mountains and a narrow strip at their base.

2020
Improvements are made to the park's Teton Crest Trail. With sections of the trail nearly 100 years old, it is one of the most iconic hikes in the United States.

1920 **1950** **1980** **2020**

1950
The park's present-day boundaries are established with the addition of the Jackson Hole National Monument and John D. Rockefeller, Jr.'s, donated land.

1988
The Greater Yellowstone Ecosystem experiences massive forest fires that burn nearly 1.5 million acres (607,000 ha), including parts of Grand Teton National Park.

2007
The Craig Thomas Discovery and Visitor Center opens in the park. Guests can come to the center and access ranger programs, view exhibits, and obtain park permits.

KEY ISSUE

FIRES IN THE PARK

Forest fires are inevitable in a park that has as many trees as Grand Teton. Some fires have natural causes. Lightning, for instance, may strike a tree and set it on fire. Many forest fires, however, are caused by human activity. A campfire may be left unsupervised. Someone might throw a burning cigarette out a window. Even the heat from a car's muffler can cause a fire.

At one time, the U.S. Forest Service had a "zero tolerance" policy toward forest fires. Whenever a fire started, a firefighting crew would jump into action to put the fire out, preventing it from spreading or causing damage. However, over time, scientists and park managers have learned more about fire and its importance to many ecosystems. Putting out a fire can sometimes cause harm to the environment in the long term.

Helicopters are often used to make water drops on fires occurring in and around Grand Teton.

Should forest fires in Grand Teton be left to burn?	
Yes	**No**
Fires are natural processes that can benefit the ecosystem. Some trees, such as lodgepole pines, need fire to reproduce. The heat from the fire helps them release the seeds needed to grow new trees.	A forest fire can devastate an ecosystem. Plant life is scorched. Waters become polluted with smoke, causing fish to die. The animals living in the forest no longer have food to eat. They are forced to move to new areas.
When forest fires are put out quickly, thick plant growth builds up within the forest. If another fire occurs in the same area, this buildup becomes extra fuel for the fire, helping it to expand in size. Fires can become even more dangerous and destructive than those that preceded them.	Uncontrolled fires pose a safety threat to people in and around the park. Fires can kill or severely injure people. They can also destroy communities and property.

Today, fire managers in Grand Teton National Park must make difficult decisions about forest fires. They must find a balance between the need for natural processes to take place, the conservation of the park, and the safety of human life. To do this, the park helped to create Teton Interagency Fire, a team of fire experts that serve not only Grand Teton, but the nearby Bridger-Teton National Forest and surrounding areas. Together, these experts monitor fire risk areas and develop action plans for each one, whether that means fighting the fire or letting it burn.

Park Attractions

One of the most popular ways to start exploring Grand Teton National Park is with a visit to the Craig Thomas Discovery and Visitor Center. Visitors can sign up for ranger talks, browse through the bookstore, and watch a movie about the park. Park staff are also available to suggest activities and sights to see.

For people who love excitement, the park's iconic peaks offer a natural playground for rock climbing and mountaineering. Scaling Grand Teton itself is a goal for many adventurers. The mountain has more than 35 routes, with varying degrees of difficulty. Grand Teton is considered a technical climb. Only people trained in proper climbing techniques should attempt to go to the top of this peak.

The Jenny Lake Scenic Drive is an option for those who want a more relaxing visit. This one-way road meanders along the shores of its namesake, providing visitors with spectacular views of the lake and the surrounding mountains. Many people like to spend additional time at the lake fishing, swimming, or boating in its waters.

The Chapel of the Transfiguration is one of several historical sites found within the park. The chapel was built in 1925 to serve the area's settlers.

Hiking is one of the best ways to enjoy the park's beautiful landscapes. Popular hikes for families include Moose Ponds and Hidden Falls. In the winter, the park's many trails offer opportunities to go snowshoeing and cross-country skiing.

BE PREPARED

Before setting off on a hike, it is important that visitors make sure they have prepared for the trip. This means bringing the supplies needed to stay safe and in good health.

Water All hikers should carry clean drinking water. Natural water sources in the park, such as lakes or rivers, often have harmful **bacteria**. People should not drink directly from a natural water source.

Rain or Shine? The weather in the park can change very quickly. Hikers should have extra clothing and rain gear on hand.

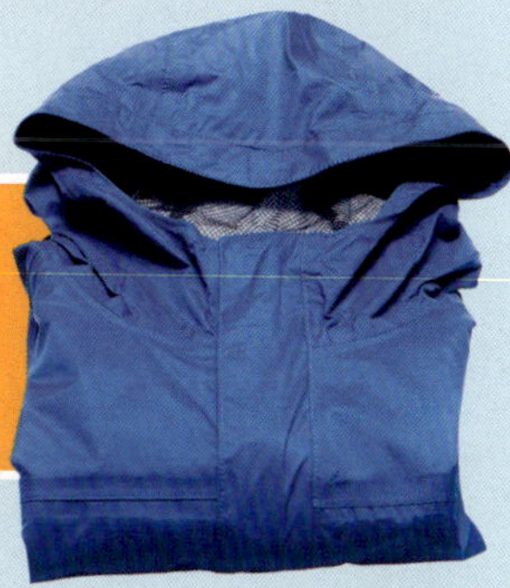

Food Hikers should bring enough food to keep energized. This will include both a lunch and snacks to eat along the way. Recommended snacks for hikers include nuts and berries.

Hiking Boots Hiking trails are known for their uneven ground. People venturing onto them should make sure they have boots with a good tread and solid ankle support.

Bear Spray There are many bears in the area, so it is important to learn about bear safety. Hikers should always carry bear spray and know how to use it correctly.

A Natural Heritage

Grand Teton National Park was established on the homeland of the Shoshone people. The Tetons have long held special cultural significance to the Shoshone. Many of their beliefs and traditions are linked to these mountains. To the Shoshone, mountain peaks were conduits to the spirit world. There, they could obtain special powers needed to help them in life.

Some Shoshone men performed a ritual called a vision quest to acquire these powers. Vision quests were often done in the mountains. A man would spend several days alone on a mountain without water or food. While there, he would enter the spirit world through his dreams. The special powers he needed would be given to him there. These powers would develop further as time went on.

The Shoshone's name for the Tetons was *Teewinot*. This word means "many pinnacles." Pinnacles are high, pointed pieces of rock.

CEREMONY AT JENNY LAKE

Today, Jenny Lake is a recreational hub. People go there to hike, kayak, and buy souvenirs. To the Shoshone, however, the lake is a sacred site. Long ago, it was where a special ceremony called the Sun Dance was performed.

The Sun Dance was the Shoshone's most important ceremony. It was held once a year, usually in late spring or early summer. Groups from different bands would gather to share in their common beliefs.

Only a few people would dance each year. They danced in order to gain knowledge or power from the spirit world. The dance itself was a form of sacrifice. It was performed over several days. Those who danced would do so for hours each day without eating or drinking.

It has been more than 130 years since a Sun Dance ceremony was held at Jenny Lake.

WHAT HAVE YOU LEARNED?

TRUE OR FALSE?

Decide whether the following statements are true or false. If the statement is false, make it true.

1. Grand Teton National Park is located in northwestern Wyoming.

2. The Teton Range is one of the oldest mountain ranges in North America.

3. The Teton Range is part of the Middle Rockies.

4. People have lived in the Grand Teton area for at least 11,000 years.

5. The Tetons are an example of fault-block mountains.

6. The highest peak in the Teton Range is called Tall Teton.

ANSWERS

1. True.
2. False. The Teton Range is one of the youngest in North America.
3. True.
4. True.
5. True.
6. False. The highest peak is named Grand Teton.

SHORT ANSWER

Answer the following questions using information from the book.

1 What types of rock form the Teton Range?

2 When did the Craig Thomas Discovery and Visitor Center open?

3 What is a fault?

4 In what part of the park did the Shoshone hold their Sun Dance ceremony?

5 How does fire help trees such as lodgepole pines?

ANSWERS
1. Gneiss and granite
2. 2007
3. A crack in Earth's crust
4. Jenny Lake
5. Heat from fires helps them release the seeds needed to grow new trees.

MULTIPLE CHOICE

Choose the best answer for the following questions.

1 Which philanthropist bought and donated land for Grand Teton National Park?

a. Franklin D. Roosevelt
b. Grover Cleveland
c. John D. Rockefeller, Jr.

2 When did the U.S. government pass the Endangered Species Act?

a. 1967
b. 1973
c. 1984

3 How many species of plants can be found in Grand Teton National Park?

a. More than 1,000
b. About 750
c. Fewer than 500

4 In what year were the park's present boundaries established?

a. 1950
b. 1929
c. 1872

ANSWERS
1. c 2. b 3. a 4. a

ACTIVITY

FORMING GNEISS

Much of the Teton Range is made of gneiss. This rock can be recognized by the multi-colored bands that run through it. These bands are formed as a result of the rock having grains of different sizes or by the separation of different minerals within the rock. Try this activity to see how gneiss is formed.

Materials

A piece of thin string

4 sticks of modeling clay in different colors

Instructions

1. Roll each stick of modeling clay into a ball. Using the palm of your hand, flatten each ball so that it looks like a thin disk or pancake. A flat, smooth work surface is best.
2. Stack the different colored disks of clay on top of each other.
3. Place one hand on each side of the stack. Bring your hands toward each other, pushing the outside edges of your stack toward the middle to create folds in the clay.
4. Use the piece of string to slice the clay in half.
5. Look at the exposed layers of clay. What do you see? How does this compare to the formation of gneiss?

KEY WORDS

bacteria: tiny living cells that may or may not be harmful to humans

conservation: the protection of things found in nature

ecosystems: communities of organisms living in the same place

endangered: at risk of no longer living on Earth

erosion: the slow wearing away of something

extinct: no longer living on Earth

fault: a large crack in Earth's crust

geology: the scientific study of rocks to learn about the history of Earth

Great Depression: a time of economic hardship in the 1930s

habitats: places where plants and animals live and grow

magma: a very hot liquid rock beneath Earth's surface

metamorphic rock: rock that started as one type but has changed to another type due to heat or pressure

philanthropist: a person who promotes human welfare

physiography: the scientific study of the natural features on Earth's surface, such as rivers and mountains

predatory: relating to animals that prey on other animals for food

sediments: materials deposited by water, wind, or glaciers

species: a class of plants or animals with common characteristics

temperate: relating to a region or climate with mild temperatures

INDEX

Get the best of both worlds.

AV2 bridges the gap between print and digital.

The expandable resources toolbar enables quick access to content including **videos**, **audio**, **activities**, **weblinks**, **slideshows**, **quizzes**, and **key words**.

Animated videos make static images come alive.

Resource icons on each page help readers to further **explore key concepts**.

Published by AV2
276 5th Avenue, Suite 704 #917
New York, NY 10001
Website: www.av2books.com

Library of Congress Cataloging-in-Publication Data

Names: Beaucage, Adrienne, author.
Title: Grand Teton / Adrienne Beaucage.
Description: New York, NY : AV2, [2022] | Series: National parks | Includes index. | Audience: Ages 10-13 | Audience: Grades 4-6
Identifiers: LCCN 2021012877 (print) | LCCN 2021012878 (ebook) | ISBN 9781791138547 (library binding) | ISBN 9781791138554 (paperback) | ISBN 9781791138561
Subjects: LCSH: Grand Teton National Park (Wyo.)--Juvenile literature.
Classification: LCC F767.T3 B43 2022 (print) | LCC F767.T3 (ebook) | DDC 978.7/55--dc23
LC record available at https://lccn.loc.gov/2021012877
LC ebook record available at https://lccn.loc.gov/2021012878

Printed in Guangzhou, China
1 2 3 4 5 6 7 8 9 0 25 24 23 22 21

042021
101320

Project Coordinator Heather Kissock
Designers Tammy West, Ana María Vidal, and Terry Paulhus

Photo Credits
Every reasonable effort has been made to trace ownership and to obtain permission to reprint copyright material. The publishers would be pleased to have any errors or omissions brought to their attention so that they may be corrected in subsequent printings. AV2 acknowledges Getty Images, Alamy, Shutterstock, and Dreamstime as its primary photo suppliers for this title.